The drawings of Edwin Dickinson

The drawings of Edwin Dickinson

with an essay by Lloyd Goodrich

New Haven and London: Yale University Press, 1963

Published in Association with The Drawing Society

A publication of The Drawing Society
1001 Park Avenue, New York City.

Library of Congress catalog card number: 63–13961

Foreword

The Drawing Society is honored to present this volume of drawings by Edwin Dickinson as the first in its proposed series of monographs on the work of contemporary artists as draftsmen. A generous grant by Mr. and Mrs. Robert C. Graham to The Drawing Society and to Yale University Press has made this publication possible.

The Drawing Society, established in 1960 as a tax-exempt organization, was conceived in the belief that drawing is the foundation of the visual arts. Draftsmanship as an armature for other art forms and as an esthetic end in itself always has been of fundamental importance. The purpose of the Society, whose National Committee consists of artists, scholars, and collectors, is to provide not only a meeting ground for experts in the field but to bring to the attention of the student and the general public the history and significance of drawing and drawings.

The Society plans to fulfill its purpose through a variety of activities. Lectures have been and will continue to be given on the various aspects and techniques of drawing. The opening talks, on the theme "Approaches to Drawing: Collector, Curator, Artist," were presented at the Metropolitan Museum of Art and have been published in pamphlet form. Gifts have been made to museums for the purchase of drawings, and it is hoped that grants can be donated to individuals or organizations involved in drawing research. The Society intends to organize exhibitions of contemporary and master drawings for circulation throughout the country. Finally, in addition to the monographs, the Society is to publish a multi-volume series entitled "The Uses of Drawing." Written by scholars in the field and edited by Winslow Ames, the books will include "Drawings for Painting," "Drawings for Theatre and Costume Design," "Drawings for Architecture," and "Drawings for Landscape."

Such are the purposes and interests of The Drawing Society. The monograph on the drawings of Edwin Dickinson is one of the first of our endeavors. There is much to come which I hope you will receive as kindly.

In closing, I should like to express the Society's appreciation to Mr. and Mrs. Dickinson, whose advice has been essential to this publication. We are indebted deeply to the owners of the drawings who generously lent them for an extended period of time in order that plates might be made from originals. The cooperation of Yale University Art Gallery and its staff in the handling of the drawings gratefully is acknowledged. Finally, particular thanks are owed to Bruce D. Hooton and Guy Luster, who saw the monograph through its initial stage, and to Edith H. Jones, who has served so ably as our editor.

JAMES BIDDLE

President

The drawings of Edwin Dickinson

Edwin Dickinson is a unique figure in contemporary American art – a traditionalist who is far from academic, a representational artist whose subjects have little to do with conventional representation, a skillful painter and draftsman who thirty years ago anticipated certain aspects of today's advanced school, a man respected equally by conservatives and avant-garde. Above all, he is an individualist, who has gone his own way without regard to current trends. He is a rare combination of classicist and romantic: a classicist in his passion for form, a romantic in his visionary content.

Born in 1891, Dickinson received a thorough conservative training, particularly in Provincetown under Charles W. Hawthorne, whom he regards as his most influential teacher. Hawthorne, an independent academician, was a genuine painter, and something of his manner lingered in his pupil's early work, which was a blend of traditional style, original vision, and unorthodox subject matter. In his late twenties Dickinson spent a year in Europe, including a visit to Spain, where he encountered El Greco, thenceforth his greatest admiration among the old masters. On his return he settled in Provincetown, living there for seventeen winters, and five more in nearby Wellfleet. Here, far from the metropolitan art centers, he evolved his highly personal art. Recognition came slowly – a few academic honors; it was not until the late 1940's, after he had moved to New York, that his position in the wider art world was established.

The Provincetown years saw the conception and completion of a series of large paintings in which Dickinson's imagination first found full expression. They created a nocturnal world in which ambiguous figures and objects, unrelated in any ordinary sense, were seen in mysterious settings and in a half-light like that of a deep forest. The objects and figures were recognizable and realistically portrayed; their ambiguity lay in their relations to one another and to their background, and the unearthly light in which they appeared. But even in this light their forms were entirely clear, painted with masterly sureness and precision. In these complex compositions the romantic and classic elements in Dickinson's nature achieved a synthesis. At this time surrealism was being launched in France, but the movement was still little known in America. Dickinson, like Ivan Albright, was an independent pioneer of that freeing of imagery from naturalistic limitations that has marked our age.

These large canvases were few in number, for he built them slowly, spending years on each. *The Fossil Hunters* took about two hundred sessions over a two-year period. *Woodland Scene* and *Composition with Still Life* occupied five and four years respectively. The more recent *Ruin at Daphne* was worked on for ten years, undergoing major changes in the process. But while not numerous, these works are among the remarkable imaginative and plastic creations of our time.

On the other hand, Dickinson has produced many smaller informal paintings, mostly landscapes. In striking contrast to his big compositions, they are usually direct impressions of nature, recorded broadly and spontaneously. Natural features are translated into simplified masses of color and tone. The free brushwork has all his painterly skill. The grayed harmonies, the soft-edged style, the unrealistic light (whether daylight or twilight it would be hard to say) create a visionary quality, even though the motifs are actual places. This blending of real and unreal conveys the sensation of landscapes seen in dreams. Whereas his large compositions present recognizable imagery, the informal paintings often approach abstraction – without, however, reaching pure abstraction. Specifically, they have parallels to abstract expressionism. Yet Dickinson began to paint them in the 1920's, a decade before the rise of the movement in this country. Although seemingly so different from his large works, they are related by their visionary character, their common source in nature, and the structural sense that underlies them.

The foundation of Dickinson's art is his sense of form. It is an inborn gift, which showed in his earliest work. In his major compositions the forms possess vitality, sculptural largeness, and richness of substance. At the same time they have refinement and precision – a combination of the large and the fine that is not often found. His sense of form is not mere academic correctness; it is a sensuous apprehension, like the more common feeling for color. He has always had a passion for perspective and its complex problems. His pictures are built with a clear understanding of their three-dimensional structure, that of round forms in space. He has a highly developed sensitivity to the relations of forms to one another, and to the space in which they exist. But the picture plane is always re-

spected – the pictorial space beyond which forms cannot project or recede without destroying the formal unity. Everything is governed by his sense of design, of the overall order and harmony of all elements.

With this preoccupation with form, it is not surprising that Dickinson loves to draw, and has done so all his life. But his drawings are not studies for his paintings; the latter are worked out on the canvas in painterly terms. His drawings have quite a different purpose; they are independent works of art. He is one of the few painters for whom drawing is an end in itself. His best drawings are as complete, within their range, as his works in any medium.

What is the special quality of drawing, as distinguished from painting? Without color, body of pigment, complex technique or large scale, drawing lacks the sheer physical power of painting. But these very limitations create its virtues. In the relative absence of physical power, drawing exists by its essential elements of form, line, and design. There are no other factors to distract from its purity.

These qualities are particularly true of Dickinson's drawings. They are never large in scale. The medium is almost always pencil, sometimes with accents in charcoal, or, occasionally, charcoal alone. There are no additional colors. Not much attention is paid to the local colors of objects, or to their textures, or to anything else that might distract from the forms themselves.

The concentration is always on form. Its character ranges from the precise and geometric to the free and fluid. In the precise drawings, line plays a leading

8

role. But its function is related to form; it does not exist for its own sake. His draftsmanship is never a brilliant linear tour de force. Nor is he a strong-arm artist, bent on surface effects. His line is one that models forms – that creates, not merely defines them. It is alive, changing constantly with the character of the forms. It is at once highly sensitive, precise, and firm. This linear sensitivity, which marks all the great draftsmen, past and present, is as innate as a sense of color harmony.

But his drawings do not depend entirely on line. Tone plays an important part, working hand-in-hand with line to model the forms. In his more precise drawings the tonality is delicate and silvery, and within a close range of values. His free-form drawings, on the other hand, are largely tonal, ranging down to deep darks.

Within these general characteristics, Dickinson's drawings vary widely, depending on their subjects, style, and period. Let us look at the various types, and at typical examples of each.

In drawing as in painting, his individuality began to assert itself fully about 1920. His studies from the nude made that year in Paris (Plates 1–4) were traditional, but by no means the regulation life-class product. Usually he included only part of the figure – the torso and legs, with the head out of the picture – concentrating on the elements that interested him. The angle of vision was often unexpected, bringing out fresh aspects of the forms. Already he was avoiding the obvious. The figure was seen sculpturally, with emphasis on its large, smooth rhythms. The draftsman-ship was precise, the line searching but sure. Often outlines were heavier than interior lines; but they were drawn after the forms were constructed – as the final definition, not the starting point. The strength of these studies was the result of first building the forms, then defining them clearly and strongly.

With the mid-1920's began some of his most original concepts, using man-made things such as houses, interiors, and objects – everyday elements selected for their qualities as form. Sometimes he chose the most unlikely motifs: for example, a motorboat's propeller, whose dynamic shape contrasts with the milder shapes around it (Plate 6). In two drawings (Plates 10 and 17) he has chosen the interior of his Province-town studio, with ordinary furniture, an old arm-chair, a pot-bellied stove. The interest lies in the dif-fering forms of these familiar objects, their relations one to another, and to the pictorial space. Everything is constructed in perspective, exactly. The extreme precision suggests mechanical drawing, but these compositions are far from mechanical. Out of the in-terrelations of forms and of space he has created three-dimensional design. One noticeable feature is that there are no pure verticals or horizontals; the chief lines are not parallel to the four edges of the paper but at varying slight angles to them. This is charac-teristic of all his drawings of this kind. Aware of the relations of all lines to their rectangular frame, he avoids paralleling the latter, by such devices as selec-tion of the viewing point or a slight tilting of the whole image. These variations from the dully regular are almost imperceptible, but nevertheless essential.

9

Such refinements create a subtle play between the main lines of the design and its frame.

One of his most complex adventures in perspective is *Staircase, the Manse at Ulysses* (Plate 12). The central motif is the line of the stairs, sweeping upward and around, in a curve of extreme grace. Just as flat pattern on paper, this curve has its own beauty; but with Dickinson nothing is ever merely pattern. The relation in depth of the spiral to the straight elements, and to the space they all occupy, the concentration on essential forms and movements, and the delicate precision with which all this is drawn make this one of his most perfectly realized designs in any medium.

A fascination with windows and what is seen through them appears in several drawings of the 1930's. The attraction undoubtedly lay in the combination of the rectangle of the frame and the varied forms outside – of the regular and irregular. In *View from Dining Room Window* (Plate 13) the interplay between the severe straight lines of the window and the exquisitely varied shapes of the snow-covered landscape has a refinement peculiarly his own. In *The Conservatory* (Plate 14) the window device is even more complete, since the whole wall is glass, and its framework creates a regular but graceful structure through which one sees the profusion of forms without. With its combined power and precision, the design has the quality of inevitability.

An odder subject is *View from a Window at Wellfleet* (Plate 24) – simply a cottage window with distant dunes and water. Here everything is asymmetrical and irregular, there is no true perpendicular or horizontal except the horizon, and the window frame leans slightly to the left, creating an unexpected linear relation to both the outer world and the rectangle of the paper. Distortion is too violent a word for this, signifying a radical alteration in objects themselves. What the artist has done is to alter somewhat the directions of the main lines, producing a slight disturbance of normal relations. Taking the most ordinary and regular feature of a house, a window, he has transformed it into an intriguing linear interplay – and also into an image with a strangely haunting quality.

Another favorite subject has been the exteriors of buildings. His drawings of Cape Cod houses suggest comparison with Edward Hopper's watercolors of them. But the motivation is different. Hopper is concerned not only with the forms of his houses but with their character, the light and weather and time of day, and the emotion evoked by the whole scene. These considerations do not seem to affect Dickinson. His houses have no particular architectural or human interest. His preoccupation is with structure, pure and simple. His precision is like that of an architect's rendering, but as always he shuns the conventionally regular. Viewing points are selected to throw all details into unusual perspective (Plates 32, 41, 45, 47). In *South Wellfleet Inn* the angle of vision is directed upward, so that the gables, towers, and dormers lean toward one another in a kind of fantastic dance. The actual inn is probably a fairly usual piece of architecture, but he has made it into something strange, almost spectral. His buildings are pictured without particularizing color, surfaces, surroundings, or naturalistic light. This exclusive concentration on geometric form produces a disembodied, abstract quality. With all their architectonic exactness, these structures have an air of fantasy, like the precise realism of dreams.

Dickinson has painted many portraits, including more than a score of himself (among his most remarkable works); and he has made many portrait drawings (Plates 15, 16, 27, 30, 33, 34, 51). Sympathetic and perceptive in their grasp of character, they are in no sense flattered, but neither are they caricatured. He does not fear beauty, especially in children and young people, yet he pictures maturity and age with an unerring eye. Often these drawings are not only portraits but complete compositions. *Esther Sawyer* (Plate 16), for example, is notable not only for the exquisite drawing of the head but for the baroque richness of the background—globe, statuette, drapery. (His love of drapery, often revealed in his paintings, is a link to El Greco.) The whole space is filled with the play of geometric and non-geometric forms. Like certain other precise drawings, this has a marmoreal severity, like sculpture in high relief, as if everything were carved out of one substance.

At the opposite extreme from his precisionist works are the landscapes he began to draw in the early 1930's (Plates 18–23, 25, 35, 42, 46, 48, 50). As the former represent the classicist in him, the latter ex-

press the romantic. Products of the free-form, spontaneous side of his temperament, they resemble his informal oil landscapes. They are based on nature and on actual places; but these motifs are transformed into broad simple masses, drawn freely and fluidly, without meticulous definition or high finish. Usually the natural features are clearly recognizable, but sometimes they can be mysterious shapes that might be trees, bushes, rocks. The light is indeterminate. Often these drawings have a dreamlike atmosphere like that of his landscapes in oil, and like the latter, are close to abstraction. But always they are filled with a sense of nature's lush, abundant life.

From the middle 1930's Dickinson's drawings tended away from precisionism toward a fuller use of tone, with rich darks, and a broader, freer style. Also in some cases there was a growing ambiguity. At this time he was painting his big *Woodland Scene* and *Composition with Still Life,* and their crepuscular mood appeared in several drawings. Indeed, the latter are even more ambiguous, for while the imagery of the paintings is recognizable, that of certain drawings presents mysteries: for example, *Nude* (Plate 26) with its dark brooding figure, suggesting Redon, or *Child in Bed* (Plate 28), where the child seems lost in the rumpled bedclothes that resemble hooded personages. In certain figure drawings he omitted some facial features, such as the mouth or nose. This idiosyncratic treatment of the face is consistent with his handling of the figure in his life drawings, and with his recurring habit of concentrating exclusively on elements that

11

interest him, and often on parts rather than wholes. But in general the elaborate ambiguity of the large oils is exceptional in the drawings, which are either more objectively formal or more subjectively romantic, and in both cases less complex.

During the last five years Dickinson has made several visits to the eastern Mediterranean: twice to the Near East and five times to Greece, including a winter in Athens. In Greece he has found a land and an ancient civilization to which he is deeply drawn. He has traveled there by ship, thus satisfying his love of both the sea and antiquity. In his drawings made on the *Tekla Torm* and other ships (Plates 52–55, 57) we see reappearing his early preoccupation with manmade objects as elements in design. These shipboard drawings have the bare purity of form that belongs to everything nautical. Never has he shown a more austere and sensitive realization of the relations between forms, lines, and space. In one of the most re-

cent, *Olympia* (Plate 57), he has selected a few elements – a railing, a mast with block and tackle, a ventilator – and out of these, through fineness of relations, variations in the thickness and weight of lines, subtle deviations from the vertical and the horizontal and from the exact right angle, he has constructed one of his most perfect designs. Substance is not insisted on; he is concerned more with relations than with material existence. This is pure creation in forms and lines – their directions, their interrelations, and the spaces they define. The rectangular grid (but not strictly rectangular) suggests geometric abstraction; but instead of flat pattern, here is three-dimensional design which at the same time creates a pattern of the utmost subtlety and refinement. Here, as in everything he draws or paints, Dickinson demonstrates that a work of art exists on several levels simultaneously.

LLOYD GOODRICH

Biographical note

Edwin Walter Dickinson was born on October 11, 1891, in Seneca Falls, near the north end of Cayuga Lake, in the Finger Lakes district of upper New York State. His father, Edwin Henry Dickinson, was pastor of the First Presbyterian Church of Seneca Falls, and from 1897 of the North Presbyterian Church, Buffalo; and a leading figure in the church in New York State. The future artist was the youngest of four children.

He studied at Pratt Institute, Brooklyn, 1910–11; the Art Students League of New York, 1911–12, under William M. Chase; and three summers, 1912–14, in Provincetown, Massachusetts, under Charles W. Hawthorne.

In 1913 he settled in Provincetown as a year-round resident, and between then and 1944 spent seventeen winters there, and then five in nearby Wellfleet. During World War I he served two years, 1917–19, in the Navy as a radio operator. After the war he studied and painted for a year (1919–20) in Paris, with visits to Italy and Spain. In 1937–38 he again painted in France – at Paris, Toulon, and in Brittany – and in 1952 at Paris and Montignac. In 1944 he moved to New York, which has since been his permanent home, with summers at Wellfleet.

In 1928 he married Frances Foley. They have two children, Helen F. Baldwin and Edwin C. Dickinson.

During his years in Provincetown he completed several major paintings, including *An Anniversary,* 1920; *The Cello Player,* 1924–26; *The Fossil Hunters,* 1926–28; *Stranded Brig,* 1934; *Woodland Scene,* 1933–37; and *Composition with Still Life,* 1934–37.

His *Ruin at Daphne* was begun in 1943 and finished in 1952.

A teacher from early in his career, he has taught at the Buffalo Academy of Fine Arts, 1916; the Art Students League of New York, 1922–23; the Provincetown Art Association, 1929–30; the Art Institute of Buffalo, 1939; the Stuart School of Design, Boston, 1940–41; the Association for Music and Art, Cape Cod, 1941; the Farnsworth Museum, Wellesley College, 1942; Cooper Union, New York, 1945–49; the Art Students League of New York, 1945 to date, except for the season of 1961–62; the Midtown School of Art, New York, 1946–47; the Art School of the Brooklyn Museum, 1949–58; Pratt Institute, 1950–51; the Dennis Foundation, Dennis, Massachusetts, 1951; the Skowhegan School of Painting and Sculpture, summers of 1956 and 1958; and as visiting instructor at Cornell University and Columbia University in 1957, and at Boston University in 1961.

As a painter, his recognition in the general art world began in the late 1940's, with articles in the art press, and his inclusion in The Museum of Modern Art's "Fifteen Americans" exhibition in 1952. His large retrospective exhibition at the Graham Gallery, New York, in 1961, established him as a major figure in contemporary American art.

Elected an Associate of the National Academy of Design in 1948, he became an Academician in 1950. In 1956 he was elected a member of the National Institute of Arts and Letters, and a vice-president, 1958–60. In 1961 he became a member of the American Academy of Arts and Letters.

From 1959 to 1963 he made two visits to the Near East and five to Greece, spending the winter of 1961–62 in Athens.

The National Academy awarded him its Second Altman Prize in 1929, its First Prize for Portrait in 1949, and its Second Altman Prize for Landscape in 1958. He received a Grant for Art from the National Institute of Arts and Letters in 1954, and a $10,000 grant from the Ford Foundation in 1959. He was awarded the Medal for Art of the Century Association in 1956, and the Brandeis University Creative Arts Awards Medal in 1959.

He is represented in numerous private collections, and in the following public collections in the United States: Atlanta University, Atlanta, Georgia; Bowdoin College Museum of Fine Arts, Brunswick, Maine; Albright-Knox Art Gallery, Buffalo, New York; The Art Institute of Chicago; Andrew Dickson White Museum of Art, Cornell University, Ithaca, New York; Museum of Art, Montpelier, Vermont; The Metropolitan Museum of Art, New York; The Museum of Modern Art, New York; National Academy of Design, New York; Sara Roby Foundation, New York; Whitney Museum of American Art, New York; University of Nebraska Art Galleries, Lincoln, Nebraska; Yale University Art Gallery, New Haven, Connecticut; and Museum of Fine Arts, Springfield, Massachusetts.

List of plates, with notes

All inscriptions on the drawings are in the artist's hand.
Numbers which do not refer to the date of the drawing are the artist's own catalogue numbers.
In dimensions, height precedes width; inscriptions are written horizontally unless otherwise indicated.

1. *Standing Nude*
   "E W Dickinson / Chaumière Paris 1920 / No. 80"
   upper left corner

2. *Seated Nude*
   "E W Dickinson / E.W. Dickinson / Paris 1920"
   lower right
   "42 Paris"   lower right corner

3. *Standing Nude*
   "83 E.W. Dickinson 1920."   lower left
   "Paris"   lower right edge, vertical

4. *Seated Nude*
   "E W Dickinson / Chaumière Paris / 1920 82 / Paris"
   lower right corner
   "E W Dickinson 1920." upper right corner

5. *Victory of Samothrace*
   "Paris"   lower left edge
   "E W Dickinson 1920."   lower right edge

6. *Propeller*
   "E.W. Dickinson 1921."   lower left
   "84"   center bottom within composition
   "Henry from / Dick."   lower right corner

7. *Reclining Nude*
   "45"   center bottom of sheet
   "Dickinson / 1923 / New York 1923"   lower right
   edge, vertical

8. *Horse of Selene*
   "Horse of Selene / 85"   "E W Dickinson
   Washington 1924 / from a plaster in the Corcoran"
   along lower edge

9. *Counter, Schooner Levuka*
   "E W Dickinson 24"   center bottom
   "To Dick & Belle 1925"   along lower right edge
   "E. W. Dickinson"   upper left edge, vertical

10. *Studio, 46 Pearl Street, Provincetown*
    "46 / good portrait of the studio EWD about 1926
    46 Pearl St"   along bottom edge
    "E W Dickinson 1926."   center right edge, vertical,
    within composition

11. *Souvenir of the Fossil Hunters*
    "E W Dickinson 1927. / To Barbara Brown Souvenir
    of the Fossil Hunters."   lower left
    NOTE: Barbara Brown, now Mrs. Philip C. Malicoat,
       posed for Dickinson's painting entitled *The
       Fossil Hunters*, 1926–1928, collection
       Whitney Museum of American Art,
       New York

12. *Staircase, the Manse at Ulysses*
    "E W Dickinson 1928."   upper left corner

13. *View from Dining Room Window*
    "To Ansley / E W Dickinson / 1930"   lower right
    corner

15

14. *The Conservatory*
"E W Dickinson 1931 / Buffalo" lower left corner, vertical

15. *Mother and Child*
"E W D   Pat Cambridge / 24 May 1931" center upper edge
"Helen" above child's head, lower left

16. *Esther Sawyer*
"To Esther /" lower right edge
"E W Dickinson / Buffalo 1931" upper right corner, vertical

17. *Studio, Provincetown*
"1933. E W Dickinson" lower left, vertical, within composition

18. *Long Point Light*
"Long Pt. Lt." lower left edge, vertical
"E W Dickinson 1933" along lower right edge

19. *Summer Morning, Beach Point*
"E W Dickinson 1934   Pat & Helen Beach Pt / Summer morning" along center left edge

20. *Truro*
"Pat & Helen / E W Dickinson / Pamet 1934" lower left, vertical, within composition

21. *Lake Shore, Sheldrake*
"E W Dickinson Sheldrake 1934 / Pat / & Helen" along left edge
"To F. J. W. & Mother Waugh; / in grateful exchange: 'The Missa Solemnis' " lower right within composition

22. *Charles W. Hawthorne's Garden*
"E W Dickinson 1935" upper left, vertical, within composition

23. *Rocks, Ontario*
"Ontario" upper left, vertical
"E W Dickinson" lower left

24. *View from a Window at Wellfleet*
"Wellfleet" lower left, vertical, within composition
"E W Dickinson 1935" along right edge within composition

25. *Woods*
"H. Graney   E W Dickinson 1936" left edge, vertical, within composition
"To Ansley" lower right corner

26. *Nude*
"1936 E W Dickinson" center right edge, vertical

27. *Rose*
"E W Dickinson / 1936." lower left, vertical, within composition

28. *Child in Bed*
"Constant"   "E W Dickinson 1936" along left edge
"Provincetown" upper right edge, vertical

29. *Male Torso*
"E W Dickinson 1936" center right edge, vertical
"56" center bottom

30. *Portrait*
"1937   E W Dickinson"   left edge, vertical, within composition

31. *Cottage Window*
"Cottage   Dickinson / Wellfleet 1939"   left edge, vertical, within composition

32. *South Wellfleet Inn*
"Wellfleet"   lower left
"1939"   center bottom
"E W Dickinson"   lower right

33. *Noel Weiss*
"E W Dickinson"   upper left edge, vertical
"Buffalo 1939"   center right edge, vertical

34. *Mary Weiss*
"Buffalo 1939   E W Dickinson"   along right edge

35. *A View up Cayuga Lake*
"Sheldrake / 1939"   lower left corner, vertical
"E W Dickinson"   right edge, vertical

36. *Sleeping Woman*
"E W Dickinson 1940"   lower left
"E W Dickinson"   upper left edge (very faint), vertical
"1939"   upper right corner (very faint), vertical

37. *Child's Chair*
"Child's chair   EWD 1860"   lower left edge, vertical
"Wellfleet 1943   E W Dickinson"   along right edge

38. *Rose and Sextant*
"1943   E W Dickinson"   lower left, vertical

39. *Cupid and Psyche, Metropolitan Museum of Art*
"E W Dickinson 1944"   center left, vertical, within composition
NOTE: The drawing is of the sculpture by Auguste Rodin: *Cupid and Psyche*. c. 1893. Marble. Metropolitan Museum of Art, gift of Thomas F. Ryan

40. *Power House, Consolidated Edison Company*
"E W Dickinson 1944 / 350 E 33"   lower right edge, vertical, within composition

41. *Van Cortlandt House*
"Van Cortland (sic) House / E.W. Dickinson / 1944"   lower right, vertical, within composition

42. *The Mall, Central Park*
"1944 / E W Dickinson"   lower left corner

43. *New York Public Library*
"E W Dickinson 1944"   upper right edge, vertical

44. *Sculpture Fragments*
"E W Dickinson / 1944"   center left edge, vertical, within composition

45. *Hampshire House, Central Park South*
"Central Park So."   lower left corner, vertical
"E W Dickinson / 1944"   center right edge, vertical, within composition

46. *Central Park*
"Central Park"   center left edge, vertical, within composition
"E. W. Dickinson 1944"   upper right edge, vertical

47. *Dormer Window, Sheldrake*
"Sheldrake"   center left, vertical
"1946"   lower left, vertical
"E W Dickinson"   lower right edge, vertical

48. *Fallen Tree*
"E W Dickinson / Sheldrake 1946"   lower left edge, vertical, within composition

49. *Reclining Figure*
"E. W. Dickinson / 1947"   lower right
"E W Dickinson / 1947"   center right, vertical, within composition
Indistinguishable name   lower left within composition

50. *Sheldrake Yard*
"E W Dickinson Sheldrake"   left edge, vertical, within composition

51. *Portrait*
"E W Dickinson Westport / 1956"   upper left, vertical, within composition

52. *Off Algiers, Tekla Torm*
"E W Dickinson"   lower left, vertical, within composition
"1959"   lower left of center, vertical, within composition
"Off Algiers"   upper right corner, vertical

53. *Tekla Torm, Porthole*
"1959"   center bottom, vertical, within composition
"Regards to / Bill Middendorf / M/S Teckla (sic) Torm / E W Dickinson"   lower right, vertical, within composition
" E W Dickinson"   upper right corner

54. *Mediterranean*
"Mediterranean / 1959 E W Dickinson"   left edge, vertical, within composition

55. *Tekla Torm*
"1959"   center left, vertical, within composition
"E W Dickinson   Tekla Torm"   right edge, vertical, within composition

56. *Byzantine Museum, Athens*
"Byzantine Museum"   right edge, vertical, within composition
"E.W. Dickinson / Athens 1961 59"   lower right corner

57. *Olympia*
"E W Dickinson / Olympia"   lower left, vertical, within composition
"62"   lower left edge
"1962"   lower right, vertical, within composition

58. *Kerameikos Cemetery, Athens*
"E W Dickinson / ΚΕΡΑΜΕΙΚΟΣ 1962" upper right, vertical
"73"   lower right corner

The plates

Plate 1

Standing Nude

Paris, 1920

Pencil, 13⅛ x 10¼ inches

Collection the artist

E W Dickinson
Chaumière Paris 1920
#80

Plate 2

Seated Nude

Paris, 1920

Pencil, 12¼ x 10¼ inches

Collection the artist

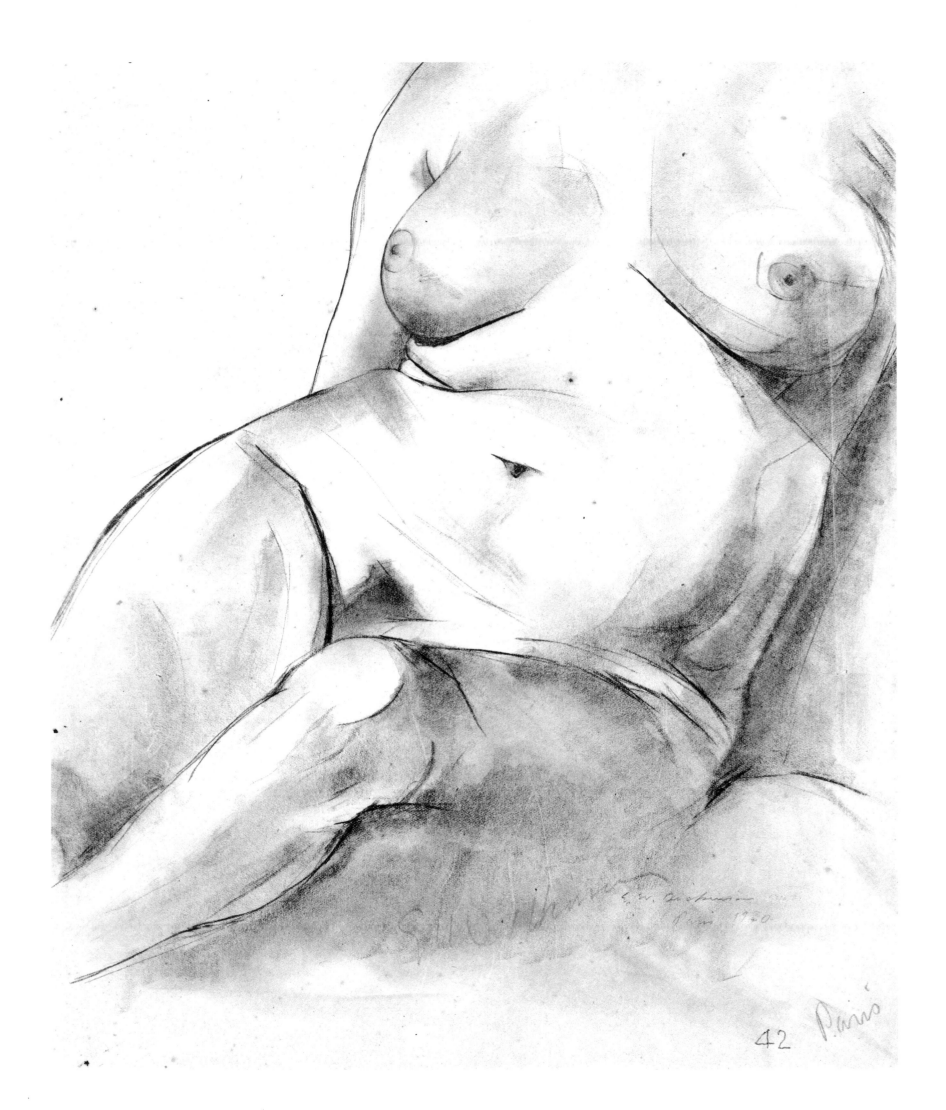

42 Paris

Plate 3

Standing Nude

Paris, 1920

Pencil, 13⅛ x 10¼ inches

Collection the artist

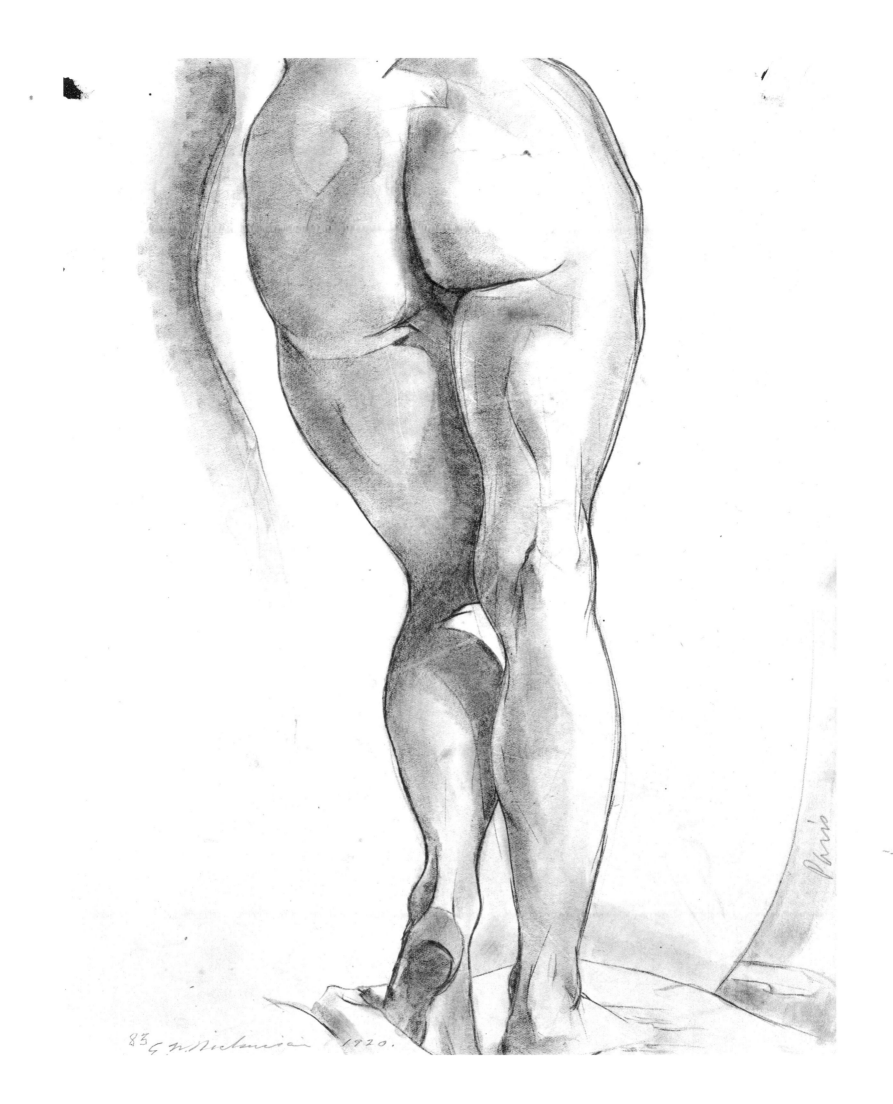

83 G.W.Nicholson 1920.

Plate 4

Seated Nude

Paris, 1920

Pencil, 13⅛ x 10¼ inches

Collection the artist

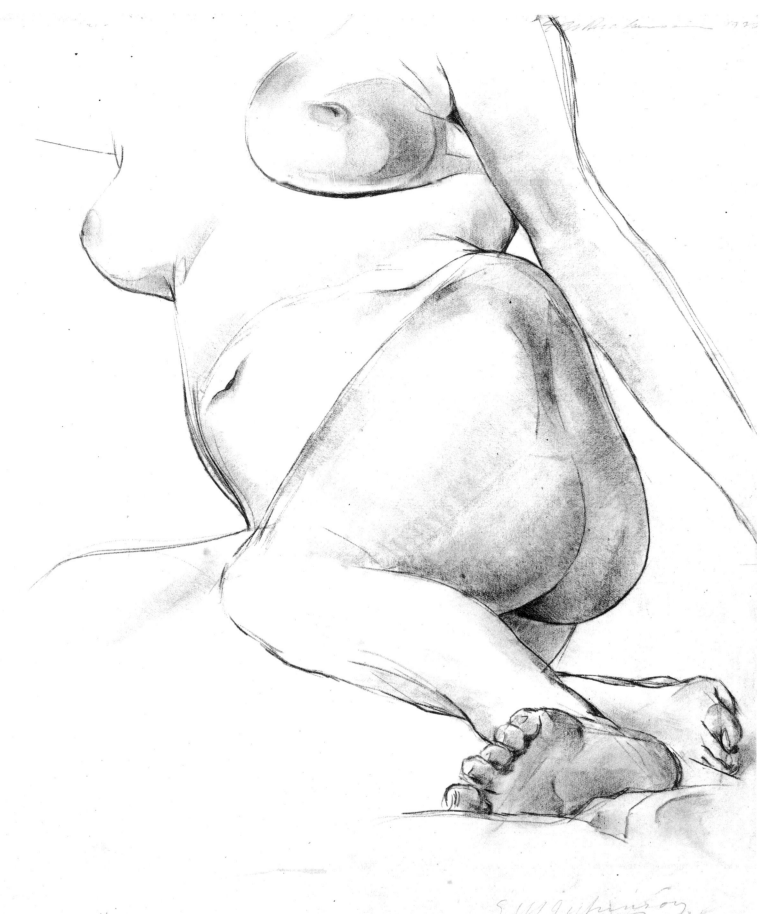

E.W.Dickinson
Chaumière, Paris
1980 82

Plate 5

Victory of Samothrace

Paris, 1920

Pencil and charcoal, 13 x 10⅛ inches

Collection Mrs. Roderick Potter, Buffalo, New York

Plate 6

Propeller

1921

Pencil, 13⅛ x 10¼ inches

Collection the artist

84

Plate 7

Reclining Nude

1923

Charcoal, 24½ x 18¾ inches

Collection the artist

45

Plate 8

Horse of Selene

1924

Pencil, $13\frac{7}{8}$ x $9\frac{7}{8}$ inches

Collection the artist

Horse of Selene
85   EW Dickinson Washington 1924
from a plaster in the Corcoran

Plate 9

Counter, Schooner Levuka

1924

Pencil, 10 x 8 inches

Collection Dr. Richard Parmenter, Ithaca, New York

Plate 10

Studio, 46 Pearl Street, Provincetown

1926

Pencil, 18⅞ x 12½ inches

Collection the artist

46

Plate 11

Souvenir of the Fossil Hunters

1927

Pencil, $7\frac{5}{8}$ x $9\frac{7}{8}$ inches

Collection Mrs. Philip C. Malicoat, Provincetown, Massachusetts

Plate 12

Staircase, the Manse at Ulysses

1928

Pencil, 10 x 7¾ inches (sight)

Collection Mr. and Mrs. Robert C. Graham, New York

Plate 13

View from Dining Room Window

1930

Pencil, 12⅜ x 9¼ inches

Collection Mrs. Ansley W. Sawyer, Buffalo, New York

Plate 14

The Conservatory

1931

Pencil, 9 x 12½ inches (sight)

Collection Mrs. Walter Lord, Buffalo, New York

Plate 15

Mother and Child

1931

Pencil, 12½ x 9⅜ inches

Collection Mr. and Mrs. Jan Hird Pokorny, New York

Plate 16

Esther Sawyer

1931

Pencil, 12⅜ x 9⅜ inches

Collection Mrs. Ansley W. Sawyer, Buffalo, New York

To Mother –

Plate 17

Studio, Provincetown

1933

Pencil, 7 x 4¾ inches

Joseph H. Hirshhorn Collection, New York

Plate 18

Long Point Light

1933

Pencil, 9⅜ x 12½ inches

Collection Dr. Richard Parmenter, Ithaca, New York

Plate 19

Summer Morning, Beach Point

1934

Pencil, 9⅜ x 12¼ inches

Collection Mr. and Mrs. Ferdinand H. Davis, New York

Plate 20

Truro

1934

Pencil, 9⅜ x 12½ inches

Joseph H. Hirshhorn Collection, New York

Plate 21

Lake Shore, Sheldrake

1934

Pencil, $9\frac{3}{8}$ x $12\frac{3}{8}$ inches

Collection Coulton Waugh, Newburgh, New York

Plate 22

Charles W. Hawthorne's Garden

1935

Pencil and charcoal, 14 x 9⅞ inches

Joseph H. Hirshhorn Collection, New York

Plate 23

Rocks, Ontario

1935

Charcoal, 8½ x 11⅝ inches (sight)

Collection Furman J. Finck, New York

Plate 24

View from a Window at Wellfleet

1935

Pencil, 10¾ x 12¾ inches (sight)

Collection Chauncey L. Waddell, New York

Plate 25

Woods

1936

Pencil and charcoal, 10 x 13 inches

Collection Mrs. Ansley W. Sawyer, Buffalo, New York

Plate 26

Nude

1936

Pencil and charcoal, 13 x 11 inches

Joseph H. Hirshhorn Collection, New York

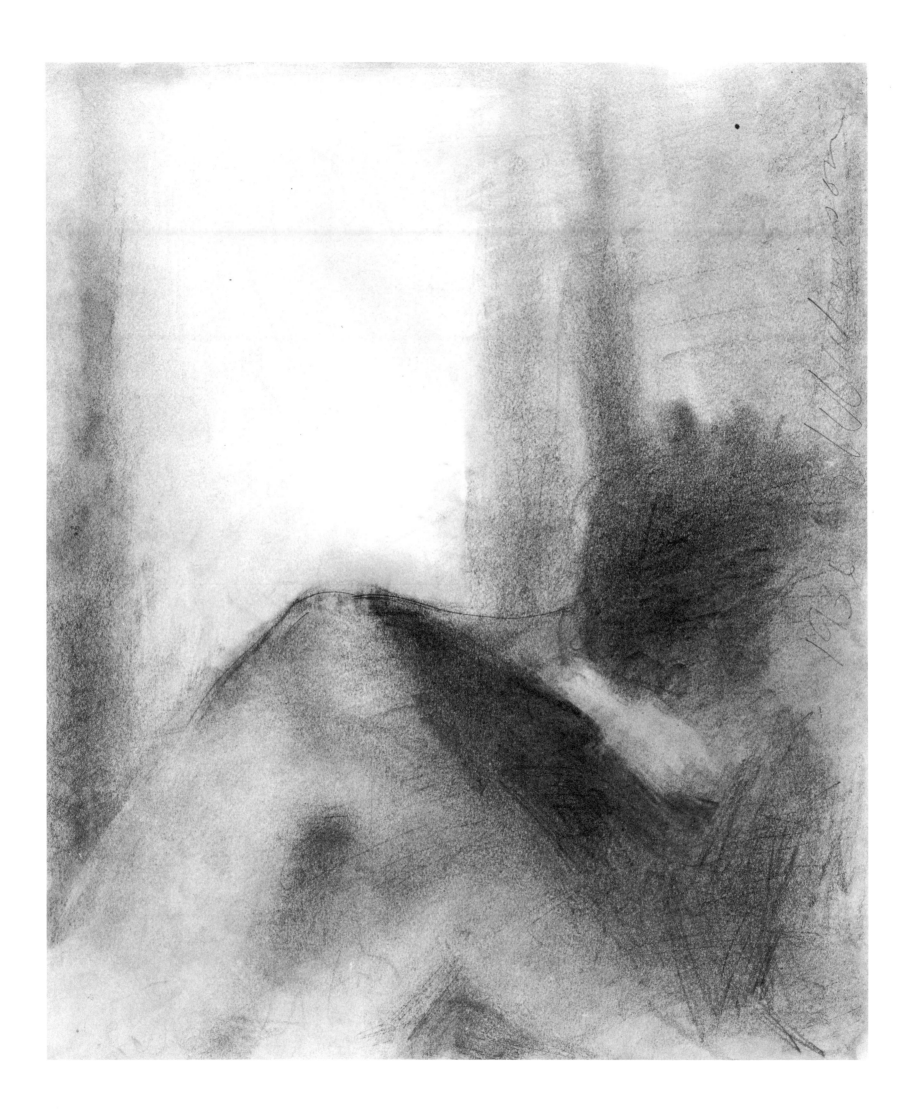

Plate 27

Rose

1936

Pencil and charcoal, 10⅞ x 12⅞ inches

Collection Mrs. Ansley W. Sawyer, Buffalo, New York

Plate 28

Child in Bed

1936

Pencil, 10 x 13 inches

Joseph H. Hirshhorn Collection, New York

Plate 29

Male Torso

1936

Pencil, 13 x 10 inches

The Graham Gallery, New York

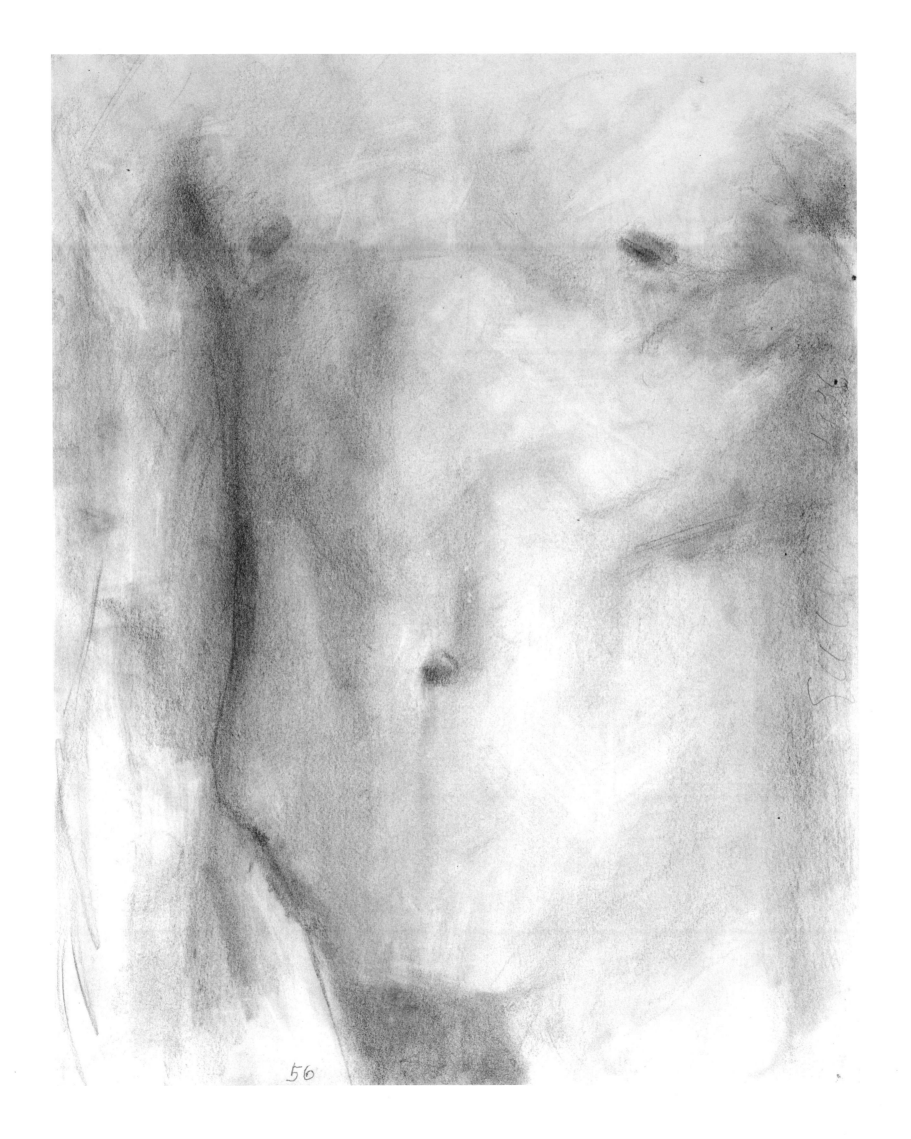

56

Plate 30

Portrait

1937

Pencil, 10⅝ x 12⅝ inches (sight)

Collection David Daniels, New York

Plate 31

Cottage Window

1939

Pencil, 10⅞ x 12⅞ inches

Collection Atlanta University, Atlanta, Georgia

Gift of Mr. and Mrs. Chauncey L. Waddell

Plate 32

South Wellfleet Inn

1939

Pencil, 8⅝ x 11⅞ inches

Collection Atlanta University, Atlanta, Georgia

Gift of Mr. and Mrs. Chauncey L. Waddell

Plate 33

Noel Weiss

1939

Pencil, 12⅞ x 10⅞ inches

Collection Edwin Weiss, Buffalo, New York

Plate 34

Mary Weiss

1939

Pencil, $12\frac{7}{8}$ x $10\frac{7}{8}$ inches

Collection Edwin Weiss, Buffalo, New York

Plate 35

A View up Cayuga Lake

1939

Pencil, 8⅜ x 11⅝ inches (sight)

Collection Chauncey L. Waddell, New York

Plate 36

Sleeping Woman

1940

Pencil and charcoal, 11 x 13 inches

Joseph H. Hirshhorn Collection, New York

Plate 37

Child's Chair

1943

Pencil, 11½ x 9¾ inches

Collection Chauncey L. Waddell, New York

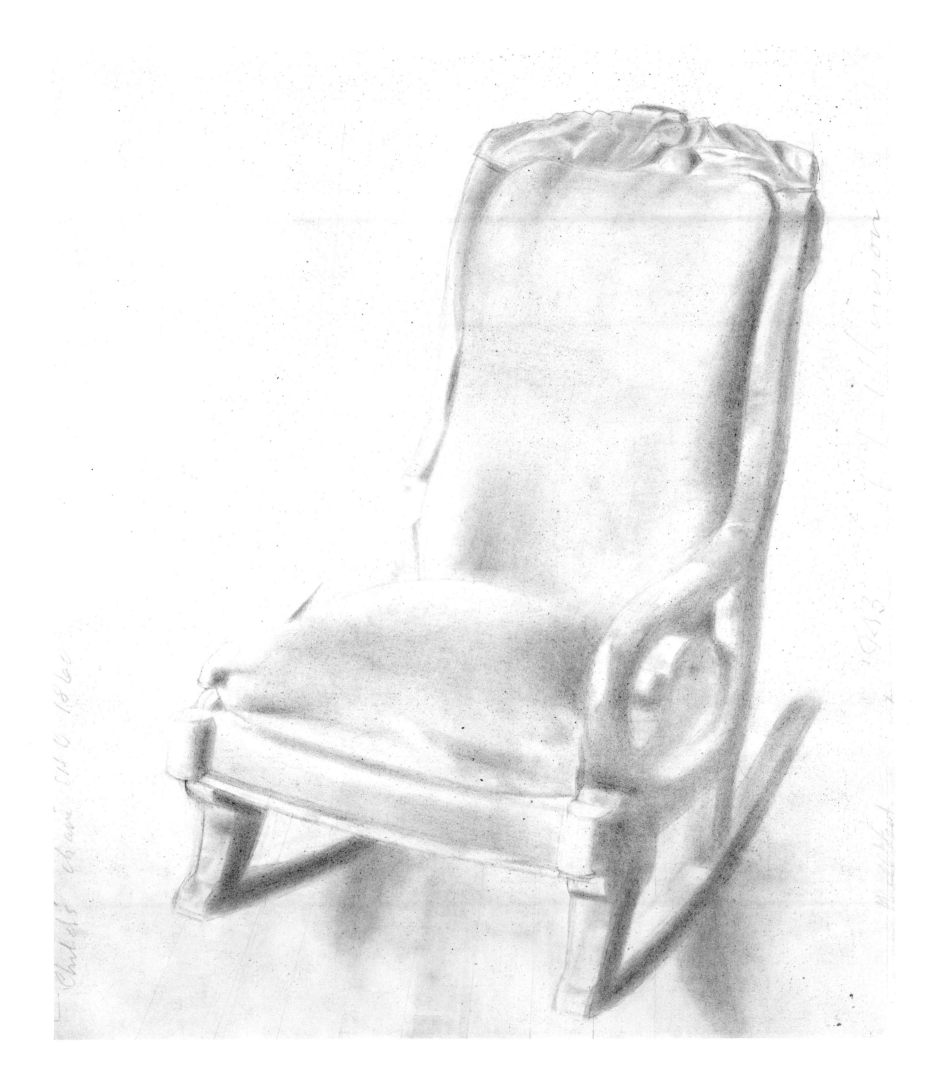

Plate 38

Rose and Sextant

1943

Pencil, 8⅝ x 11⅞ inches

Collection Mr. and Mrs. Gardner Jencks, Washington, D.C.

Plate 39

Cupid and Psyche, Metropolitan Museum of Art

1944

Pencil, 12½ x 10⅛ inches

Collection Isabel Bishop Wolff, New York

Plate 40

Power House, Consolidated Edison Company

1944

Pencil, 12⅜ x 10 inches

Collection Isabel Bishop Wolff, New York

Plate 41

Van Cortlandt House

1944

Pencil, 12½ x 10¼ inches

Collection Isabel Bishop Wolff, New York

Plate 42

The Mall, Central Park

1944

Pencil, 12½ x 10 inches

Collection Isabel Bishop Wolff, New York

Plate 43

New York Public Library

1944

Pencil, 11⅞ x 9 inches

Collection Isabel Bishop Wolff, New York

Plate 44

Sculpture Fragments

1944

Pencil, 12½ x 10 inches

Collection Isabel Bishop Wolff, New York

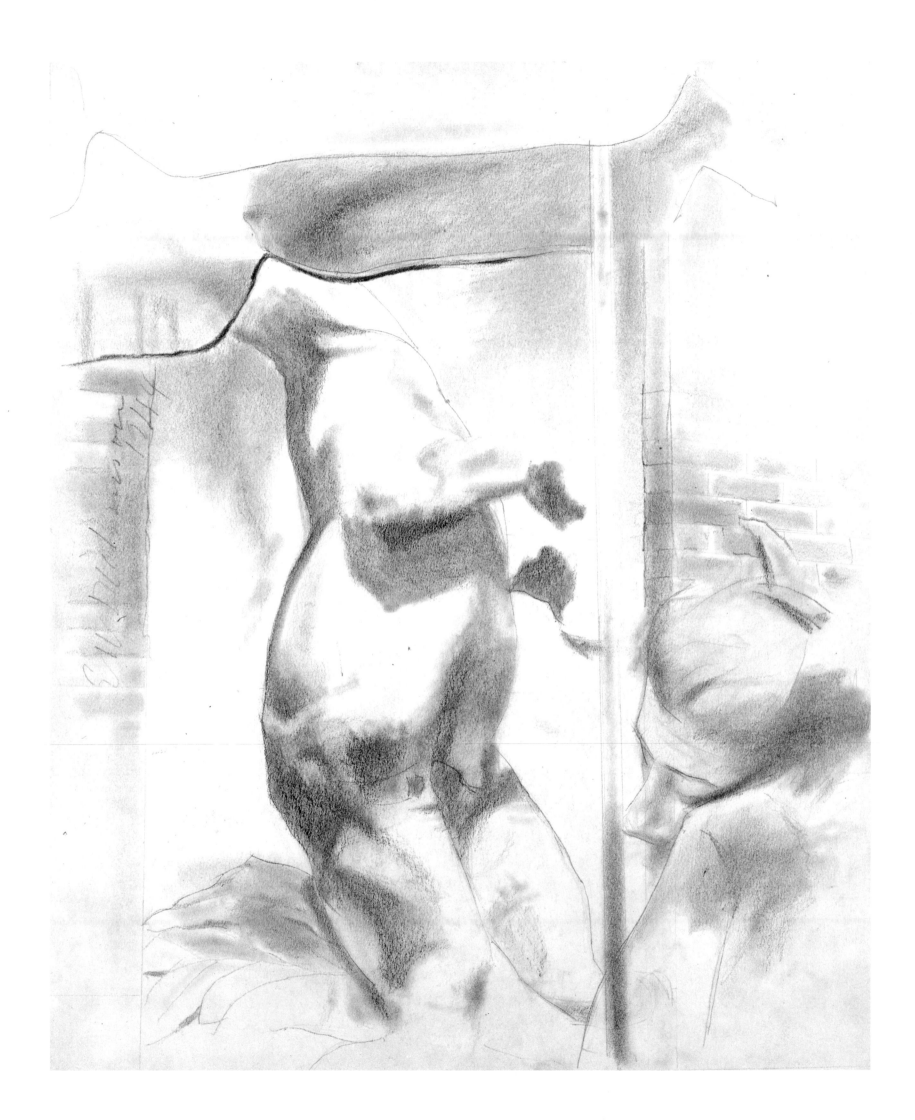

Plate 45

Hampshire House, Central Park South

1944

Pencil, 12½ x 10 inches

Collection Isabel Bishop Wolff, New York

Plate 46

Central Park

1944

Pencil, 12½ x 10⅛ inches

Collection Isabel Bishop Wolff, New York

Plate 47

Dormer Window, Sheldrake

1946

Pencil, 11⅜ x 9½ inches

Collection Chauncey L. Waddell, New York

Plate 48

Fallen Tree

1946

Pencil, $11\frac{1}{2}$ x $9\frac{3}{8}$ inches

Collection Mrs. William T. Gossett, Bloomfield Hills, Michigan

Plate 49

Reclining Figure

1947

Charcoal, 11⅛ x 14¾ inches (variable)

Joseph H. Hirshhorn Collection, New York

Plate 50

Sheldrake Yard

1952

Pencil, $8\frac{5}{8}$ x $11\frac{1}{4}$ inches (sight)

Collection Miss Dorette Oettinger, New York

Plate 51

Portrait

1956

Pencil and charcoal, 10 x 12 inches

Collection Guy Luster, New York

Plate 52

Off Algiers, Tekla Torm

1959

Pencil, 9 x 11½ inches

Collection Mrs. William T. Gossett, Bloomfield Hills, Michigan

Plate 53

Tekla Torm, Porthole

1959

Pencil, 9½ x 6⅜ inches

Collection J. William Middendorf, Jr., New York

Plate 54

Mediterranean

1959

Pencil, 11½ x 9 inches (sight)

Collection Mr. and Mrs. Robert C. Graham, New York

Plate 55

Tekla Torm

1959

Pencil and charcoal, 11½ x 8¾ inches

Collection Dr. and Mrs. Milton M. Gardner, Merrick, New York

Plate 56

Byzantine Museum, Athens

1961

Pencil, 8¾ x 11 ¾ inches

Collection the artist

59

Plate 57

Olympia

1962

Pencil, $9\frac{5}{8}$ x 12 inches

Collection the artist

62

Plate 58

Kerameikos Cemetery, Athens

1962

Pencil, $11\frac{3}{8}$ x $9\frac{5}{8}$ inches

Collection the artist

73

Designed by Alvin Eisenman